THE SEVENTH TOWN OF GHOSTS

THE SEVENTH
TOWN OF GHOSTS

Poems

FAITH ARKORFUL

McClelland & Stewart

McClelland & Stewart and colophon are registered trademarks of
Penguin Random House Canada Limited.

Published simultaneously in the United States of America.

Library and Archives Canada Cataloguing in Publication data is available upon request.

ISBN: 978-0-7710-0445-2
ebook ISBN: 978-0-7710-0446-9

Cover design by Emma Dolan
Cover images: (leaves) Hand drawn Chinese mandarin orange. Original from Biodiversity
Heritage Library. Digitally enhanced by rawpixel; (space) A runaway star, called CW Leo,
plowing through the depths of space and piling up interstellar material. Original from
NASA. Digitally enhanced by rawpixel; (hand) Emma Innocenti./ Getty Images

Typeset in Adobe Jenson by Sean Tai
Printed in Canada

McClelland & Stewart,
a division of Penguin Random House Canada Limited,
a Penguin Random House Company
www.penguinrandomhouse.ca

1 2 3 4 5   28 27 26 25 24

Penguin
Random House
McCLELLAND & STEWART

CONTENTS

THE SEVENTH TOWN OF GHOSTS

"I'm giving up on land to light on, and why not,
I can't perfect my own shadow, my violent sorrow, my
individual wrists."

— DIONNE BRAND

ORIGIN STORY

it was a dream we entered through
beaded curtains the night my mother
fell asleep and awoke wrapped
in a blanket of stars as delicate as a spider web.
i am going to tell you about yourself, she says
which means she is going to tell me what she knows of
a beginning for herself. my mother sings to me in words
saved for worship as we watch the sun and moon
coalesce. as she speaks, the sky holds
itself together for a moment. my mother hands
me a grapefruit that we siblings
split into three pieces
and that is as far back
as we can count kin. this is the end of that story.
the flesh pulls apart in my hands like a
yawn in a quiet room. she wraps her hands every year
around her face and closes her eyes, insisting stars
into calendars.

masking itself as cherry. Bark expanding
not unlike the ridge where knuckle meets finger.
There is a lie in my yellow nails and in every word
stuck under my tongue. I can say I want to be alive
but today that feels like a betrayal too.

It is not mandatory to want to tie myself
down to the earth. Reunite with all my family
resting on the ocean floor. I did not forgive.
Time found its own rhythm. I rejected that angry
and terrorizing precision. I watched my nails grow.
I told my sisters I love them.

I've started braiding ragweed into my hair
trying to keep myself puffy and swollen
and of the earth. Otherwise I begin to gamble
the prospects of distant hydrangeas.

I have woven my own death into a currency of
existence. One part of my will remains in the grave
and the other scratches at the door.

I am valuable because I am. In the lagoon smell and
green blur into one. There are no hierarchies made
of air or luck or determination. I wait for the splitting
moment. For my body to expand enough to let the night in.

is it right to escape yourself before
someone else can decide for you?

nothing fits the same when you're gone.
to drink   a glass of water
becomes work.   sitting still becomes
work. moving is nauseating. i spin   myself
in circles trying to create   in my bedroom
the passage of time   the earth's orbit.
the moment you exchanged your body
for fog   i stole every dream i ever
had underneath my mattress. i want to say
i was hiding for safekeeping but
really i had left   for the mice.
i could no longer trust myself   to remember
the good.
all i have now   is the kingdom of growing pains.

My people. A guess.

My name, a shiver indexed
as a breath. The woman who
raises my father like her own
has a different machination.
This eruption is beneath the
waves and beyond category.

If I hold before you a knife in one hand resting
against somewhere precious and in the other,
a cup? I lose every time. To know a drinker is to know
advanced mathematics.

One exercise:
> Taking into consideration trajectory and pitch, at what moment
> does the sour haze of a breath intersect with my shadow, hiding
> from your heaviness?

I study collisions so often I become one. And your collisions become
my curses. Death to the breath that burns. Death to the debate I
will always lose. Death to the promise of change made in the morning.

There have been moments where I,
watching your heavy swaying body sleeping after an eruption,
unable to tell the difference between sleep and stillness, have asked,
What vexation is this?

They say in the beginning there was nothing. But in the beginning there was
a struggle. A noise. All your weight connects with the earth, you are impossible
to lift. There was I, putting you to bed fully clothed, removing only your shoes.

You show me a drink that you pour into your hand before lighting it aflame.
Your hand is bright and burns. For a second, this is our life, burning
and in the smoke you cannot see me. Your voice after many years of
drink has become a flame grasping at all the air around it.

And it is only your voice I can hear. And it is to this voice I leave my last curse.
To the voice that asks *Can you hear me?* I will always say yes.
Yes, I can hear you. I will hear you even when you are dead.

QUIET TIME

I like two places
the nightclub and movie theatre.
People gather full and
without the expectation to talk.

I work through the times where the night
tries to eat itself.
I love the night even when it's bright out.
I call this silence. All power to the people,
to the bump and grind, to my partner's
laugh at a good joke
in the middle of the film. All power to
those who belong to the fury of togetherness,
which cradles everyone.

I have considered the earthworm
and that I am a part of the dirt
stuck to the earthworm swooped up
into the mouth of a bird and that disappears
again and again and again and once more
and for millions of years an earthworm still has
no interest in teeth and
all the interest in carrying five hearts.

I am so obsessed with proving
this. We are a single potato growing
out from another potato,
held together by a flower at the stem.
If I give up on this, I give up on it all.

I think about all the people who ruined me
just by knowing me. I seek to not know
anyone. Why would I want to get to know
anyone? At this hour? I don't think lowly
of you. I don't study you. I know enough
people now. I listen only if my sisters have a joke
to tell me. I grew a big list of disappointments.
I am shaped like a slinky. Organs slipping down the stairs.
Now nobody has to know me now. No body to know.

THE SEVENTH TOWN OF SELF-SACRIFICE

Vengeance is the silent virtue.
I shred myself with my own hands.
This sharp annihilation toward myself.

My grief is a presence
with no middle.

I have never been betrayed
by my want, my ask, for silence.

VULTURES

the subway is a place for my gods, naturally.
underground, prayers are caught in
the tunnels and stay there. we hear the
fragments of lost devotions moving
between the stations. magma flows through
me, a bubbling desperation. i so quickly transform
pain can't keep up with the shifts.

i never get what i want. i can only hear
devotions in my room. no wishes granted for
the non-existent. there is no room to create
a love that is not willing to hold through the season.

autumn is a season of handcuffs, handholding
and scarves i can't tie. i am learning now

of escape. when i say i love to be alone i mean that
i let the cold take me, i let myself become
a part of its breezes, its heaving shallow
breath felt against the mouth. i open,
i ask no questions. you must pretend to be

pitch black. vultures forming a prayer circle
wider than the moon. no call.

VACATION

And on the third day we went to Grand Etang and I
was still alive. Death digs its way into every vacation
and in this homecoming
I grow larger. Canada, my body, a frozen lake.
This lake was poured into a volcano
stuck between many answers.

And for a brief moment I can see
what could be the entire history of me. My ancestors
bussin ah wine on the mountain and swimming
on the lakebed and with teeth like sugarcane splinters scrape
the last bricks of the old church. Other strands, more mundane
are not allowed together
and fade without cure.

A black girl learns to worship herself very early. Tends her own burns.
To hide in the dark. After we return from Grand Etang
I realize I want to have it.
I.
I want
without my body having to give in to the water.
I want
all the love
I have for myself.

Let's throw salt on old and new, all the ghosts
pretend
call for sun and water
love beyond all interruptions

CONFESSION

forgive me   it has been more years than creases
in my hand
since i have had a sip from a cup of my own.

there is no
country for this black girl
in tenderness   no nectar poured into my mouth
no rubbing of feet or head

i don't yearn for it as much as i question
what it means that no one will   offer themselves
after many lifetimes reborn   each time with the same face

i had convinced myself in anxiousness that
the reason people avoided my gaze
was due to my ugly disposition   a swollen face stuck permanently

but it was a lie. what had happened
was that in each migration of my life
a ghost stood behind me waving their arms
behind my head. you can see it   once

i have chosen to show you.

the spirits are easier to explain   than how a life without
a sweetness in the air keeps me too stuck
to the earth   drags me out of my bed
no goal loud enough to
silence the drowning that happens inside myself

watch like so.
i find you not listening.
take like so.
move quick.
there's no time to write.
there's no time to take
measurements. allyou
have never touched salt.
allyou know nothing in
your hands.

to learn to cook from my
mother is to grow all of one's
knowledge underneath
your hand. no fungi can
make its own food. they live off
cells, both living and dead,
growing until the source
becomes something
resembling the quiet of
a bush that chooses
who to speak to and when.

I like simple things. I can't understand most sports because I stumble past their rules, make up my own. My only rule for basketball, for example, is to never lose your own voice from screaming. If someone else's voice disappears, the game was good.

Formula 1 is not hard to understand. Ode to the fastest person or the fastest car. How I learned to be cruel or how to braid the perfect plait. I've learned racing to understand most things in the world: observe, *observe*.

I like that there's only twenty drivers. No massive roster of giant recycled men, just a small world. And this world is a powerful machine.

The car moves forward, nothing to linger in the past. And there are so many days I need to be brought into the next day, dragged along. I feel. Sometimes I need to scrape. To crash and run out of the fire. The gust that breaks upon your skin as something rushes by. A spark on the asphalt.

I look at my cousin. We are webbed beyond our shared grandmother. Closer, siblings. Both, first-born. We are our fathers' firsts. The most vulnerable voracity of a first-time father flattens our runway. Look, accept his enthusiasm and constant discipline. We have memories of the family as one thing. The memories we cannot remember we rewrite; imagining the family as happy. Our siblings hate us for the power we hold. Equal parts god and child and king. But I howl a loud noise that frightens. My cousin does not. He keeps the sadness between his eyebrows. He keeps the sadness always.

When I was a child I wrote a play
with a regular family with a regular dad
and regular mom who did not know
the prerequisites of violence.

I never knew alcohol to be
a depressant. I see the way
it sets fire to people, makes them
too trusting of the light.

This is a play without an ending act
the suffering
feels like a dark endless moon.

Forgive my surprise I lived
beyond this regular play. That I pointed my head
looking for a star, for the cardinal and
the comfort.

Remember that story you wrote,
that the pages were blank, that when I read the lines
aloud no sound came out. That no one remembers
the childhood you had but you.

PASTA

All day I think about pasta.
All day I think
All day

I have to eat. I have to wheat.
I don't want to speak when I eat.
I want to move without a sound
under layers of sauce using
the shared breath of this world.

If only, I imagine, I make so.

How did it feel when your sister made herself into a ghost?

    I felt nothing and I mean it. It was better for everyone.
How so?

  We won the lottery and were able to retire and settle early. In the
floorboards of her bedroom were bands and bands of cash. And like
Jesus could make so, could duplicate each night. I want for nothing.
No one spoke of my sister thereafter. I forget her name sometimes.

I would love to tell you this ruined me and it was something she
anguished about, this very idea, her own ruining of my own ruining
might stain the lives tied around her. What prevented her for years
and years and years and years and years and years and years and years
and years

Fills a room
of crushed petals and
rosewater. I want nothing
else than to be sustained
by saltwater. All I want
is to trim it, this survival, until
nothing is left to remember
to ache and chase the memory of.

My mother and I desire for a second coming.
Of those who survived. My family likes
that we found our kin on the ocean
floor and on daytime reruns.

One woman tells another that her loved
one is a spirit and does not want hurt.
Does a thief know what it's like
to put their weight down?

Mami lived one hundred summers
and on the day of her centennial walked
into the orchard.

I have no answers, only small honesties.
The moon moves around us and us around
the sun. Every breath a plant makes is an
act of forgiveness. Winter is a chore and a
punishment. I know these truths.

Mom has ocular
melanocytosis and in these spots she keeps
her spirits trapped. They stay silent as we
watch. The widow on the screen shakes

like she is contemplating leaving
her body. Mom has never been easily impressed.

I laugh until my own spirit contemplates
this address. A suitable place for residence.

MIRACLE BABY

Auntie has three children and all are born before breath.
She takes the third child home. She lays him to rest in a crib
he'll never grow out of.

———

Miracle baby. Gabriel opts out of making an appearance,
but men of the earth are always willing.
The rudest carries a machete. He chops at the ground
looking for weeds and finds cousin's hand.

One palm carries a long scar through it, an oblique,
undiscovered constellation.

———

Where is my cousin?

How does one find a rib?
My mother and her sister go silent.
Auntie shows me
how to make sorrel instead:

Just boil the sepals of roselle
like so. Add sugar to taste.

———

A rule, unspoken:
Drink to keep the mouth
and mind occupied. The blood cool.

i.

father / my only father / no one believes me when i say you are in my
life / i am always weaving you into existence / without prompt / into
all conversations / this work is not a position i took willingly / i have
tried to separate the part from the whole / you and i / it is work to
escape my splintered self / that part of me / the same parts of my
being / i tried to dissect with a bushel of lavender

ii.

father / in the daylight i became more drastic / i tried to peck at what
parts of me weren't you and / i have done all this / just to escape my
splintered self into the forest / why would anyone want a body /sitting
beside on an empty bus to prove a point / who wants a body that has
to keep making a point / who wants a body that has to prove itself

iii.

father / the last time i tried to leave / i took on the life of a small bird
back home the chickens sleep in the trees at night / my splintered self
was always better at talking about death / making it funny /a punch-
line that never gets tired / my splintered self says to be kind / that to
myself we speak / from wherever the hurt found a way in

iv.

father / my splintered self and my mother are talking / my mother
tells my splintered self she would never go to the funeral of someone
who has rejected life / no exceptions. / i watch this conversation from
the window / from the tree in front of my house

v.

father / on the eve of my last day as a bird / a man plucks me from the branches / if it is you who finds me i cannot tell / a man plucks me / if it is you or it is me who leaps / you have already been forgiven / if it is you or me or you / i cannot tell / a man plucks me / his large lovely hands around my neck / says a small prayer / and

"And if I make this Earth a metaphor I make a metaphor against the police"

—MIGUEL JAMES

JUSTIN TRUDEAU DREAMS IN BLACKFACE

The Booster Club Minstrel show on the evening of St. Patrick's Day was an artistic and financial success. The audience was so large as to completely fill the hall, and, indeed, many had to stand throughout the performance.

—THE WELLAND TELEGRAPH (MARCH 20, 1908). WELLAND, ONTARIO.

"I am wary of being definitive about this because the recent pictures that came out, I had not remembered."

I am wary of this parade of a body not mine. Kidding! Kidding? Not kidding. Where to put this face, wipe clean what is no longer mine. No longer running and circling for fun. I dream of the body that is large and scary and real wild and fuckable. The pleasure is in wiping it off sometimes. I go home to run. I paint in grease and ash and oil. This country belongs to me. This body, all bodies. I am a kingdom of bodies. Indeed, many will have to stand throughout my performance.

MY MOTHER EXPLAINS TO ME WHAT A ZOMBIE IS (WHILE EXPLAINING HER JOB AFTER A LIFETIME OF MINIMUM WAGE TO HER NEW CO-WORKER ON THEIR FIRST BREAK OF THE DAY)

No nightmare worse than the everlasting body that is made to work byforce, oh.

Was it polite when the cops disappeared
a man already gone from
his soul? Their dominion bleeds a dead red hue
over maps, over sleeping boys, over numb
girls explaining every winter how
ancestors are their perennials
on this island. We go to jails aware
we might not return. We plan burials
the way citizens here apologize:
through repetition. We grieve for the moments
paper seems not to award us. We rise
like ghosts but the voice is whole and clear.
Sorry carries the privilege of pretend
to a battle. A wound that cannot mend.

They say the bingo hall is haunted. My uncle's face appears on the face
of every gambler. I count them with a dot marker. I spend months
startled by double takes, mouth agape, drooling pools onto the
pavement. These pools that follow me home and try to strangle me.
Please make your way to the back to collect your prize. A yellow dab,
the luckiest colour, a star in the sky.

In the morning I become good at approximating times. This is how
thirteen minutes pass without you. This is how I sit in a chair for
seven minutes without you. This is how I bring a slice of fruit to my
mouth without you. I teach myself for an entire era all without you.
The very first curse was life. Eighteen sunsets without you. I wait.

Every gala is sour, too bright,
cruel, too willing to kill, kill, kill, can't freeze.
Every bite is rotten, a soft chew that cannot
be sliced.

I cry. I claim that my connection
to my people is not there. Have you even
tried to connect. Truly have you ever
actually tried. I ask a ghost how and they
lead me to a tree. I touch it and the plant
begins to hum. You see? The ghost tells me.
You must listen first before you speak.

On the front:

"I feared for my life."

"I feared for my life." "I feared for my life." "I feared for my life." "I feared for my life." "I feared for my life." "I feared for my life." "I feared for my life." "I feared

my life."

for

for my life

my

red   life

I feared for

only I feared   getting   caught

I feared I only feared getting   my life my life

all mine I feared I

If you say a word long enough it becomes nothing. It means nothing.

It is deep into the season and this Kimberly is on her fifth face of the summer. Her faces can live independent. Great if they could mind their business. Instead, four faces follow in their favourite ways. No one behind them in a store, not by a company trying to make money off the latest trend, definitely not by the beast. They morph and slide out of handcuffs. A camera shutters. Our best friends are black so it's okay. My best friend is black so it's okay. The four faces burn in the shade. The four faces cover the spot the tanner missed. Have you ever opened up an orange, stuck your thumb in the navel and found your finger lodged deep in an eye? It's what she deserves. Jumping through hoops, keeping it very gucci, losing her earrings at the bottom of the sea. On the bottom of the sea, the dead use lost artifacts as currency. The first face doesn't speak. The third face said I should be grateful. The second face said that I *should be flattered*. The fourth face told me I was being too mean. You black girls are always complaining. Fix your face. I wish I could. I wish that I was reaching. I wish I could put my hands in the heavens and graze fingers with all the dead.

COUNTDOWN TO A NEW FACE

"It seems like everywhere I go I can't get real love,"
says Kim. Why'd she go on and do that to herself

I am asked. Why would she destroy her face, I am asked
as though beauty is only alive. Let the dead keep their eyes

open if they want to. The old face is a reminder.
The old face is because of you but it is only

for her. What you wanted is exactly what we both
got. To make yourself a way out of things you can control
when they mark you for the things you cannot.

I tried to explain the story and you said that if
the police don't provide a reason for the stop then they
have done something illegal. You are telling me this means
I am allowed to walk away. I am trying to explain that
I have never seen a police officer struggle to find a reason.
You and I do not share the same rules. My father's head sinks
into himself repeating the words that come before he's flung
into the earth. His golden hum cannot mend them.
The words of a beast are fragmented.

> *Where are you going.* I am not finished talking to you.
> *Buddy, where do you think you are going.*

A man is resting
all his weight on his gun. Wonder what he
means by finish. I am touching the gash in my father's
forehead. A ripe and open ackee. I will touch a man's hands
while waiting for the bus and he will tell me his friend was killed.

I will not say
Oh really. I will say
I know.

Listen, it's hard to walk away with your head still whole.
Empire suffocates itself. You are telling me something about
apples. About fruit rotting among the bunches. You are telling me
this like you are the first person to tell it. I tried to explain that
they called him buddy before. The casual friendliness
of a forward-facing beatdown. You think I am lying. Over-exaggerating.

Heavenly body, they love to punish you just as much as they
love to watch. We are gathered here today to tell you. Our country holds
my head under the water. Our country is no
different. You've heard it all. About the weather.
I hear your country is nice. That the people are real polite.

WHAT ERA WOULD YOU TRAVEL TO IF YOU HAD A TIME MACHINE?

a) a little to the left
b) two steps to the centre
c) not over there
d) n/a

I can only guarantee my breathing in the present. This life is my only chance. What comes before glows in the dark. These ghosts had little time to dream about me. They might say, *Go. Go* on with yourself.

they say we are a family good at extending / i make a decision to hold
a seminar on how to live / i schedule this party for my uncles on the first

day of spring / my dead uncles play hooky with the afterlife
slipping out of their graves while the ground unthaws / the earth still soft

i could never play hooky myself / all my childhood my mother kept her
hand wrapped around my wrist / a lightweight shackle held me

down all nights / a weight my mother gifted me for my own sake
the taste of iron swirling in the mouth always / no shard of a
coconut to scoop out the pulp of the night.

my dead uncles arrive to the seminar an hour late / they hover above
the chairs in my backyard / my living uncles arrive after the dead ones
and the reunion is a big family affair / my uncles orbit around one another

and me / with haste / all the seminar pamphlets are
out of my hands / papers with titles: / interactions with cops
explaining health complications to your doctor / drinks with bitters

my uncles hand me back this polite literature / they insist upon
an idea that in the afterlife / there is no time for posturing over

anything other than perhaps a garden / someone you love deeply
the truth of it they insist / is that most of living you never really learn

the police come through / as they always do / breaking the warmth
of the reunion / my uncles sit together around a table playing dominoes

the police lean over and ask to play / the police lean over to claim
that someone has called about the noise / the police are leaning over

What noise, I ask. Half of the people here are dead. / my dead uncles
do not speak in the presence of force / is that not what you wanted
this is the living of not knowing and wanting more / survival at

the cost of pride / now that the police have arrived the party
must end / my dead uncles / must return to the earth
before night / when the ground hardens / and although the party

starts late / it ends late / if not as late as we wanted / but still
i feel so loved / i hold all my uncles together / they hold me
in the spring we get used to the sun / staying for long

my favourite void is from the valley of lateness / i love lateness
i love it like i love my uncles / my late uncles / my late late uncles

alive and dead / oh, how i love / the suggestion that the earth
can extend / that there will always be room for more.

Stretch your mouth out to make a perfect circle. When that fails, make a quiet groan. Pull your nails out. Pull your nails out. Front a train. No, crawl inside the tunnel. There are tracks and there is your head. She was going and no one was going to stop her. Bite the dog back. Bite the dog back on its neck. I don't know how to flush away the cursed road without risking a flood. Almost all of these funny animal posts are staged. Bite the owner.

When he's frustrated my father says my hands shake like the house did when Ivan arrived. A monster ripped the roof right off the top of his wife's house. A gardener pruning the bulb of a tulip. A house he would not visit if only to make a point. The wild dogs that run the island spend their days sunbathing and telling bad jokes. When I'm not feeding strays, I spend time wondering if the madness followed me here or if I brought it with me.

The moment before the sun rises I feel a weight
on my chest. I reach out in the dark
and find my own hand at my neck.
Deep sleep moves like death.

The sun is up. I open my mouth
and the weight says *Be afraid if you want.*
I say, *Are you a friend* and the weight says, *I am
half-revenge, half-dirt sitting under
your bed.* That's not all that helpful, I think
but I say nothing.

The weight says, *I am allowed out only as
you sleep* before lifting an eyelid and jumping
back into my body.

The spirit above my head, it knows
how to gut a fish, cut off fingertips
and hooves, chops the head cleanly off.

As water through the earth, this spirit
flows through me. Blood becomes water,
and in the centre of the lake I am always red. My baptism is
in water and fire. Continue. The exorcism is daily.
I writhe on the floor, claw at my face
and soon beg for nothing. Not even the afterlife,
swaying above me, its own small town.

The flood

was

the beginning of an interminable

offing   in the luminous space

the tide seemed   red   with

A haze   that ran out to sea   . The air   above

condensed into a mournful gloom   motionless over the

earth.

We   affectionately watched

nothing that

resembled   trustworthiness   It was difficult to   not

.

Between us there was   the bond of   our

yarns   and

convictions.   the best

lying   brought

the bones.   leaning against the

sunken   ascetic   with his

palms   outwards   .

We exchanged a few words lazily.   there was silence

For some reason   we   begin   We felt

nothing

Watch for the gap. There is no shadow
that doesn't follow. No shadow
that does not block out some space
within the name it has been called.

To police: social or communal organization. *Obsolete.* To police: what arrives in the night in the form of a hyena or a large shadow cast out of the mouth of a tyrant. To police: the forecast of a tornado. Take two options: not here, or safe. To police: no de-escalation. To police: everything in blue. To police: blue uniform. To police: blue-bruised. To police: blue lights on the concrete. Today we are alive, tomorrow. To police: *but what are you going to do when you have a problem who will you call then, hmm?* To police: I called you and I was killed. To police: I am called for and killed.

Imagine the alpine swift, which spends days upon days suspended in the air. Imagine only one half of your brain allowed to rest at a time. The other half, always on alert. Left to work and watch for predators. I can tell you that I call for no one except my own voice: a chirp after days and days of migration. The alpine swift can go months without touching the ground. To police: I will come home alive and stay that way. To allow the earth to work slowly. To lord, to find something, absolutely anything better to do. To allow a bullet to melt.

I am followed only out of suspicion.
I still love the city, regardless. I get real low.
There is a loveliness here, even if it's heavy.

1. the thing about death is

2. there is no killing myself

18. and sometimes it is enough to
carry me into the morning.

3. and my siblings are fine with it

17. i sit with this buzzing mind

4. there is no killing myself

16. i sit with this game

15. i sit with this

5. and my friends are all good.

14. only has wickedness
to offer

6. all of life is connected

13. i refuse to believe this
good world

7. like how extracting the
heart of palm is what
kills the tree

12. the earth confesses to me its
wickedness but offers me its
delights

8. like how a pair of shears
kills the crab

11. this good world
this good world
this good world

9. so there's no dead and

10. i do not deeply miss this world

I AM THE CENTRE OF MY OWN LIVING

I AM THE CENTRE OF MY OWN

I AM THE CENTRE OF MY

I AM THE CENTRE OF

I AM THE CENTRE

I AM THE

I AM

I

I

I AM

I AM NOBODY

I AM NOBODY ELSE

I AM NOBODY ELSE BUT

I AM NOBODY ELSE BUT MY

I AM NOBODY ELSE BUT MY OWN

I AM NOBODY ELSE BUT MY OWN BECOMING

WHAT IS THE CENTRE IF NOT JUST YOUR ACTIVE
    ATTENTION

In the night my uncle returned
from the farm which in itself is
a miracle. Some men fall from trees and
never get back up. I watch generations
grow and die in the harvest season.
Uncle returns each year a little
weaker and just as poor. Cheap apples
don't fix the road. He brings a barrel of fruit
and my mother gives him my old phone.
Beetles flee from flame and I am a roach
shaking away from the light,
digging into a rotten apple,
eating the core and all the seeds.
For the best six months of the year Canada
steals my uncle away to dig in the earth.
No secret here. One night I was born and
ever since I have had the smaller power
to argue if only in a louder pitch.
I do not use this shaky power.
The constant reaching
upward to pick fruit shreds
lineages like a game of tug-of-war. We play
for keeps, for life. I do not use this shaky power
because I do not know how to use it. I do not
use this shaky power and all the fruit is
worthless.

"my veins don't end in me
but in the unanimous blood
of those who struggle for life"

—ROQUE DALTON

It is very easy.

Difficult things:

Tectonic plates, the evolutionary progression
that led to the existence of the modern botfly,
making risotto, assembling furniture.

But you! You are so easy.
There was no fight. There was you, and all
the moments before. In front of me, only more time and this miraculous world.

This miraculous world of the botfly, this miraculous world of warmth,
all of it grows within me.

Inside of me,
inside of us all is a distance.

But when I am held by you
the entire world becomes close.
All things attainable. All things are possible.
All things are divine. All the things are mine.

I WISH I COULD BE LIKE MY FATHER

who swallowed all his hatred
for a world never known as his. I memorize a story
to recite when people ask where I came from:

One morning, on a very regular day, a regular man (ordained
as so) saw my father's radiance and cracked his head
wide open on the curb of a sidewalk.

How could I be accused of lying when you
killed anyone who could prove otherwise.
I caught the holy ghost in a lie.

Since I crawled out of his head
he is convinced he owns me.

But if I am born out of a head
then I am born out of myself.

i will not take a snack from the pantry just yet but i want one now; no one wants to be the first to the food; if i open a treat immediately then someone will eat afterwards; which leaves less for me the next time i want more; it's all in the timing. in this house; open late at night when it's quiet and no one will see; hover like a creature over the sink; open the box from the bottom; repeat until caught; pour a drink and measure with your finger the ounces of liquid; be prepared to answer; *who drank all the juice*; say; if a snack is your favourite you are allowed to eat more; some foods are meant to be eaten by certain sisters; my sisters; after twenty-five years my mother is retired from parenting; when we fight over food she waves her hand from the couch; eyes unmoved from a scratch ticket; leave me alone; allyou monsters are allyou have; and she means it.

BOUNTIFUL

I wish I could say that I worked
hard for the happiness I have today but so much of it was a gift.

And so yield to everything.
I yield to the crushing weight of living
I yield to spit
I yield
I give in all the reins to this joy
I know what it's like to
savour in the aftertaste, to know of a
sweetness only remembered, already gone.

I hold all the good days recklessly. The ones
where I pick flowers off the ground and with

the salt and brine of my hands I preserve them.
I keep the petals in my palms for brewing later.

I want to move away from moments where a
voice that sounds like mine says:

Come through and get over it. Get like me.

Sometimes my undoing voice confuses
the voice remembering songs from the early aughts.

I need to remember that my life is sticky. That all
living is mourning. That spiders don't crawl into
the mouths of sleeping people.

My breath lives on in the bottoms of the lungs of
those who loved me.

I thought when I died I would go alone so
I lay down to hear the eternal burning.
I felt nothing but a
sun-warmed earth. So untrue to go alone.
For me, for you. Something always follows.

THE SEVENTH TOWN OF NIGHTS

is where I learn that the sunset and
I are one. The king of the second town
is both a shadow and the structure,
with a head that drips of heat and
limestone. When someone asks me to
name myself I bring the night.

MOLOSSER

The jaws of a molosser hold a myth
of permanence. For eleven years I kept
my hand in the dog's mouth waiting for
the rumour to exist in real time. When a
child asks for a dog they are asking for
an encyclopedia on love.

Gave him a birthday, a world
forced to keep notes on the bewilderment
of his life

When dad came home with the dog she looked
into his giant glassy eyes, convinced he crossed the water
to torment her by chewing up her shoes.
In Bylands, she went barefoot on Sundays, god's day.

Somewhere my love grows
in absence. Bereavement busies the body
with bizarre hallucinations.

Did you know a ghost dog never stops
barking, even when you command
it otherwise?

to my mother's hands   part sunbeam   part cutlass
a woman digging into the soil
                finding in the pasture

treasure we bring to the pawn shop
                we exchange for gold rings.

she greases her hands   with oils that warm the skin
wraps each finger in yellow yarrow

the same hands that fed me   that rub my face
        in the cold

she wears stacked rings
                on each finger.
years later, i am grown enough to be
grown.   i mirror my mother   i cascade into her

duller in colour
                unable to believe myself
to curse
until i tip my head back   back to her again

to her holding me   parting my hair with her sharpest finger
kneading dough   to her pointing at the selection on the wall

telling me to pick a rouge for the month.

years later i am asked   are those yours
when people look at my hands.

explain to me   how it could be otherwise.
everything that is on my body   is mine.
everything that is on my body belongs.

DISHCLOTH

The father subscribed to the gradual
method of cleaning after himself in small
portions. Scrubbing the dirt before
it has a moment to become a spot.
She, already born with a cord around her neck
more inclined to managing explosions of filth.
Building and building until
it is time to herald a new house.

There are two methods of forgiveness.
She learns to live in the peach seed of experience.
Beside her, the father steps forward
and into an underpass of no sound.

OH GOD!

My father is always speeding in his car.
I yell out, Oh god! Look out! as we weave
through traffic like a tightly woven braid.

He tells me, They need to look out for me!
He is a man who believes only two kinds
of people, family and everyone else.
And they is everyone else.

My father breaking the ankles of teenagers
at the court well into his middle age. He cradles
a ball with a gentleness that reverbs in his voice.

My father is my father but he is also the father
of all cute babies (who love him) and puppies (who
also love him). My father snores and will wake up
and tell us that he was always awake!

Such a liar! Just admit it! Just resting, he insists.
His eyes, his many eyes, heavy. Always open,
always risen. Father of all flowers in the summer.

I had no choice! says my father when I ask him
why he is my father. My face is his face, the way
the sky shares a colour with the sea.

When we are in the car we sing poorly together.
We make up the lyrics as we go. Look out!
I have to yell out all over again. Oh god! How I love him.
His joy stretches a horizon. His joy of flowers.

Of raising a child, of washing the sleep
out
of my eyes
with his thumb.

Pressure dissolving.
In my hand I once held a boulder.
All of my friends came together
to crack it open. Inside lived
a stunned hummingbird.

When they were finished we
held each other and watched
the creature bury itself underground.
My friends tell me I'm beautiful
because they know me.

in the water. The unfurling nature of sisterhood came with one condition. Sibling in the night as a side profile. A bone split in two. To be both what we could have been and will never be. Sibling stands in as reflection. Beneath us, a hole in the ground we dug with our own hands. Each of us with one hand tied behind our backs. A consonance between her right and my left. Dirt underneath the fingernails. Soil in the air.

TWO LEFTS

I want all the stories you're in.
The one where you're a plumber
or the time you won sixty dollars
at the casino and drove home.

The one, especially where you're laughing
and you never stop. Where we drove to an
apple orchard and I had to navigate.

Go left at the next exit, I say.
That's your right, you say very calmly
as we move through a hurling ball of iron.

I said turn left and pointed right. I said,
Oh, my other left. And you nodded.
And it wasn't a big deal. You even laughed.

I like you here, in this world where there
are two lefts.

Perhaps these worlds don't matter
to anyone but us, but even still I have to
say it, right here. In every world I know you, I love you.

THE SEVENTH TOWN OF GHOSTS

All my love, all my happiness,
my sweetness, was never
just spent speaking with my ghosts.

Not in this half of my life, anyway.
My happiness, my only me, was spent here.

In the night there is a call.
She will try to find reason in our
family's warm-bloodedness, in her own father's
perennial habit of disappearing and reappearing. She will
blame this all on her grandfather's voice, sticky like the
hypnotism of a slow wine.

The found objects of familial relations are not discoveries,
and more akin to unwanted gifts. As a child, she went
looking for her father and found shade under the leaves of
a fig tree. She found, among other things, a garden.
Cousin found a gun. I find, in the hollow of a lily, an
echo that sounds like: who can be blamed for this death?
The memories of relatives wreak havoc in the shadows.
This cousin's memory, like the flowers my mother clips
from this garden, is freshly cut and heavily watered.

Sometimes I touch my mouth and taste blood.

I've taught myself to reanimate the dead.
My mother runs the cutlass through the earth,
looking for something to salvage.

In the mess, cousin, I see an ecology:
limbs like tangerine flesh, bone like the
rind of an unripe lime. We are the children of a farmer.
A heart buried in a terracotta pot, the marrow soaked right through.

THE FLOWERS

I thought you would come to me in a dream.
Instead we met among the flowers. I mean, we met
at a restaurant. I watched your hands
cross the table while you spoke and imagined
I was committed to anguish. Who was going to tell me
that this world is ever changing? That my heart
which had nourished my loneliness would crave another
meal? That I knew little. That I always had more.

Let's never go back to Gravenhurst.
A town with a name like a funeral home
and less stars in the sky than promised.
I don't know how we drove through those
clouds of snow that tried to kill us in Orillia
and survived but we did it. In Gravenhurst,
our eyes never got used to the light because
people point their flashlights at the sky afraid
of even a moment of darkness.

You said let's keep going toward one supernova
expanding on to the next so we did. We took the only
star we saw home as a souvenir. Rubbed our hands in
sunscreen and plucked it out of the sky.

It burned through our palms, rattling like coins shaking in
a tall can. Driving home the star burned into the back
car seat, which was luckily covered by the insurance
we bought had we been killed by the snow in Orillia.

When we arrived home and back into the city,
we opened the doors of the car and the star
tumbled down the street and through traffic
until it began to blend in with the light of the traffic signals
reflecting against the pavement.

Forgive the beauty, for its long
and sudden call. I don't ever want to leave the city
with my sick hands even if the cure for life is being in it.

EXORCISM

I swirl the remnants of the spirit in a small cup
the bond of flesh provoking me
my dedication as possession.
I avoid eating the rind and claim only the fruit.
If he wants to drive go ahead.
If he wants to crawl into my eye then fine.

If you want to sing the gospel until he leaves go ahead.

I keep salt in my pockets to prevent
going too far into
the wickedness that flowers
half of yourself.

I take long subway rides to hide from god
where the reception underground is
a barrier from the echo of prayers.

My family made of pyrite
of the smoothest stone.

In 2005, they discover Eris, a plutoid whose mass
surpasses Pluto's by twenty-seven percent.

Upon discovery (or perhaps, better said, knowness),
the existence of Eris regulates Pluto to plutoid status.

Eris, of strife, of disagreement. The definition of
planethood disturbed. My sisters laugh and the sound creates

a planet. Every morning I go
outside, I touch, I briefly touch people who will never

know me. Over and over again, a planet.
People who laugh in the heat

of a summer, all planets. Their cheeks pressed close
against one another in the late summer, a planet

colliding with another. And it too
is a planet. I don't know you. A planet. I never
will. A planet. There are many plutoids maybe

(I don't know science!), colliding and obliterating
before knowness, before discovery, there are many

universes. You are one, a planet.
You who does not know me. You are
a planet. Feel it here. Put your finger to the page.

If not, look closely. If not, listen. If nothing, let it be
known. Let it be true for yourself as it is true for me.

i have been no place awake that is as
beautiful as the rip in the sky my sisters
grew one morning out of a holy boredom.

i am called into this tear in the sky
to the pulpit of sisterhood.
it's all love   this autumn where the sun
eases into the night
like an orange peel   curling, drying into itself.

my life is crafted for utility   my families ask me
for my help like a confession
something between fear and desperation
i put a tangerine   against my mouth
and tried not to bite. something is missed.
the want without the blood.

some mornings i awake tangled inside
a cadaver pouch made out of silk
the only task left for myself is a
dutiful rotting   a reflection of endurance
has a smell that burns

a life like a record of fractures
some survived and others just forgotten

my useful life squeaks   caught between canines
it sits on a swivel   it gives people the wrong directions
if only to make the trip longer and not end as soon.

i have never felt desired
i hold eyes for everything   all my appetite
pooled in buckets of rainwater
i dipped my head in   looking for sweetness
and tasted ash
a savoury farewell   blooming   again

LINKED

I believe that we are linked by a hum of the world.
The wind, the water, your sun.
The world is a good place.
I fumble through what I cannot
see. This is what carries me. It carries me always.

I refuse to believe this is all the world has to offer.
All things are humming beneath the surface.

the mother knows of one type of lagoon.
the kind where people dump waste that algae
eats at. i am my own lake inside an
ocean, making someone a mother. it was
far from my choice but that does not
change the outcome.

the other lagoons are small and shallow
separated by larger bodies
with walls of coral or sand. why am i
to pretend she is not already aware of this lagoon?
her eyes are salted with mirrors
my mother cuts open an apple
to find the seeds inside have begun to sprout.

there are some lagoons, i learn, where fish
can live in both fresh and saltwater.
she holds the possibility of a whole different
world inside another. if i cut open another
apple and find roots i know to be not afraid.

I sought out to live. But it's mine. I hold close this life, reach out and grasp it as it flutters and press it close to my chest, my heart beating alongside it, making a new rhythm. I suffer, yes. Yes, I suffer. And I still love nothing like I love myself. My life, stained orange like the tangerines I feed the dog. I accept this living, let a slice dissolve on my tongue, hold both the acid and sweetness. This isn't the life I sought out to live, but I thank it, I'll anoint the day in fragrance and oils, all parts of its soft and delicate shell. I am here with you, says your life. With my woes, with my woes, with my woes and all the other parts. If you're reading this, it don't end here. If you're reading this, it isn't too late.

ACKNOWLEDGEMENTS

I would like to firstly thank my siblings, Hannah and Eden, for being my best friends and the best people. My parents, who were the first people who believed in my art and encouraged me to always keep writing. Thank you.

Canisia Lubrin, my editor, for believing in this book and for thoughts and feedback that were challenging and clear and always spot-on. An editor, a mentor, an icon. It was a dream to work with you. I would also like to thank the entire team at McClelland & Stewart for their support.

Earlier versions of some of the poems in this book appeared originally in *The Puritan, Hobart Pulp, Canthius, GUTS Magazine, Arc Poetry Magazine, Peach Magazine, Prism International, Brick, CV2* and *The Fiddlehead*. I thank the editors and publishers of these magazines.

Thank you to Amos Tutuola, who inspired the title and whose writing guided me through the bush of this book.

The Seventh Town of Ghosts took a long time for me to write. Thank you to friends who let me talk at them about it for years: Axel, Margot, Julian, River.

I would like to thank my partner, Steve, for bringing so much love into my life. I heard that laugh for the first time at Banjara those years ago and since then I've never wanted to hear something more.

"THE SEVENTH TOWN OF GHOSTS" was titled from a chapter in Amos Tutuola's novel *My Life in the Bush of Ghosts* (1954).

"JUSTIN TRUDEAU DREAMS IN BLACKFACE":
The quote from *The Welland Telegraph* comes from the following text:
—Nicks, J. & Sloniowski, J. (2010). Entertaining Niagara Falls: Minstrel shows, theatres, and popular pleasures, in *Covering Niagara: Studies in Local Popular Culture*, eds. Joan Nicks and Barry Grant (Waterloo, ON: Wilfrid Laurier University Press). Page 298.

The sources below also provided additional information during the crafting of the poem:
—Howard, P.S.S. (2017). *Timeline of Canadian Blackface Incidents.* Retrieved from: https://www.mcgill.ca/aapr/blackface-canada/timeline.

—Howard, Philip. (2018). A laugh for the national project: Contemporary Canadian blackface humour and its constitution through Canadian anti-blackness. *Ethnicities*. 18(1). 146879681878593. DOI:10.1177/1468796818785936.

"COUNTDOWN TO A NEW FACE":
"It seems like everywhere I go I can't get real love" is a quote from bell hooks's 1997 interview with Lil' Kim in *Paper Mag*.

"FAMILY AFFAIR":
Is indebted to the poem "the earth is soft" by Sanna Wani.

"ARK, (THE FIRST PAGE, REVISITED)":
The lines of this poem are taken in erasure from the first page of *Heart of Darkness*, by Joseph Conrad. The following edition was used:

—Kimbrough, Robert ed. (1988). *Joseph Conrad's Heart of Darkness: An Authoritative Text Backgrounds and Sources Criticism*. W.W. Norton & Company.

"ENDLESSSSSSSSSSS":
The line "What is the centre if not just your active attention" is a rephrasing from a tweet from the poet and lawyer Chimwemwe Undi.

© Sarah Bodri

FAITH ARKORFUL's work has appeared in *GUTS Magazine*, *Peach Magazine*, *PRISM International*, *Hobart Pulp*, and *Canthius Magazine*, among other places. In 2022 she was a semi-finalist in the 92NY's Discovery Poetry Contest. She received an honourable mention at the 2020 National Magazine Awards and in 2019 was shortlisted for the CBC Poetry Prize. Faith was born in Toronto, where she still resides.